Girlology

SOCIAL MEDIA SAVVY

Facts and Figures About Selfies, Smartphones, and Standing Out

by Elizabeth Raum

CAPSTONE PRESS

a capstone imprint

Savvy Books are published by Capstone Press,
1710 Roe Crest Drive, North Mankato, Minnesota 56003
www.mycapstone.com

Library of Congress Cataloging-in-Publication Data
Library of Congress Cataloging-in-Publication data is available on the Library of Congress website.
ISBN 978-1-5157-7877-6 (library binding)
ISBN 978-1-5157-7881-3 (eBook PDF)

Editorial Credits
Mandy Robbins, editor; Kayla Rossow, designer; Kelli Lageson and Jo Miller, media researchers;
Kathy McColley, production specialist

Photo Credits
Getty Images: Alberto E. Rodriguez/Staff, 24 (Jacob Sartorius), Allen Berezovsky/Contributor, 24 (Jake Mitchell),
George Pimentel/WireImage/Contributor, 24 (Hannah Alper), John Lamparski/Contributor, 26, Kevin Mazur/
Fox/Contributor, 24 (MattyB), Paul Archuleta/Contributor, 24 (Emily Bear), The Washington Post/Contributor,
27; Shutterstock: Antonio Guillem, 22, 47, cunaplus, 44, (bottom), dboystudio, 46, DisobeyArt, 4, (left), Dots777,
38, Evan El-Amin, 25, Evgeny Murtola, 43, Fine Art, 30, (right), g-stockstudio, 4, (right), George Rudy, 17, Hogan
Imaging, 32, Iakov Filimonov, 31, iofoto, 15, Jaguar PS, 24 (Jazz Jennings), Kathy Hutchins, 24 (Amanda Steele),
Leszek Czerwonka, 20, marco mayer, 28, (bottom), Marcos Mesa Sam Wordley, 42, Matthew Corley, 29, Monkey
Business Images, 10, Nitikorn Poonsiri, 44, Top, Odua Images, 36, oneinchpunch, 37, Pratchaya Ruenyen, 8, Preto
Perola, 28, (top right), rangizzz, 13, (top), Rawpixel.com, 16, 23, Rohappy, 13, (bottom left), SpeedKingz, 40, 41,
Stuart Jenner, 30, Syda Productions, 9, Syrytsyna Tetiana, 7, Tinseltown, 25 (Kate Perry, Justin Bieber, Taylor Swift,
Rihanna), Undrey, 28, top left, vovan, 13, (bottom right), welcomia, 33

Design Elements
Capstone Studio: Karon Dubke; Shutterstock: AD Hunter, Angie Makes, Antun Hirsman, blackzheep, Bloomicon,
Mariam27, MPFphotography, optimarc, In-Finity, Bloomicon

Printed and bound in the USA.
010846S18

TABLE OF CONTENTS

Chapter 1

SOCIAL MEDIA IN OUR LIVES

Social media is your electronic communication lifeline. The majority of people on social media connect with mobile devices. What's your favorite way to stay connected?

HOW DO MOST PEOPLE STAY CONNECTED?

80%: smartphones, tablets, smart watches, and other mobile devices

20%: gaming consoles, desktop, laptop, and notebook computers

80% 20%

WHO'S ON THE INTERNET?

A better question might be, "Who's not?" The Internet is a worldwide phenomenon, but there are some places where Internet use is more widespread than others.

Internet Use by Region of the World

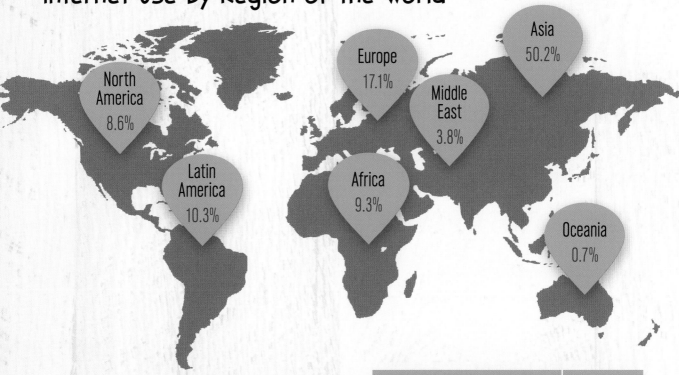

North America
8.6%

Europe
17.1%

Asia
50.2%

Middle East
3.8%

Latin America
10.3%

Africa
9.3%

Oceania
0.7%

Compare the percentage of Internet use shown above with the percentage of the world's population that each of these regions make up.

Region	Percentage of the world's population	Percentage of Internet use
Asia	**55.2%**	**50.2%**
Europe	**10.9%**	**17.1%**
Latin America	**8.6%**	**10.3%**
Africa	**16.6%**	**9.3%**
North America	**4.8%**	**8.6%**
Middle East	**3.3%**	**3.8%**
Oceana	**0.5%**	**0.7%**

WHO USES SOCIAL MEDIA?

Almost everyone! The majority of people who use the Internet have at least one social media profile.

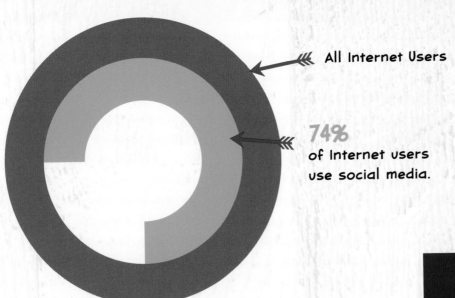

All Internet Users

74% of Internet users use social media.

Boys and girls tend to spend their time on the Internet in different ways, particularly when it comes to gaming and social media.

■ = social media   ■ = video games

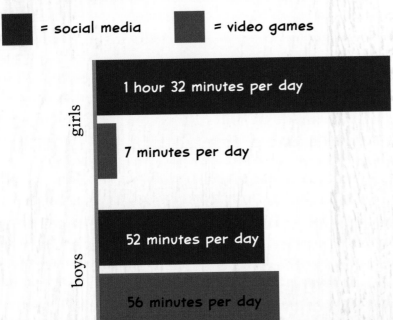

girls

1 hour 32 minutes per day

7 minutes per day

boys

52 minutes per day

56 minutes per day

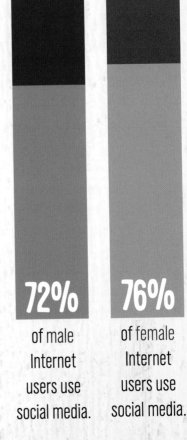

72% of male Internet users use social media.

76% of female Internet users use social media.

SOCIAL MEDIA BY AGE

Internet and social media usage varies with age.
Understandably, people who didn't grow up using
the Internet don't use it as much as younger people.

Percentage
of people on
social media

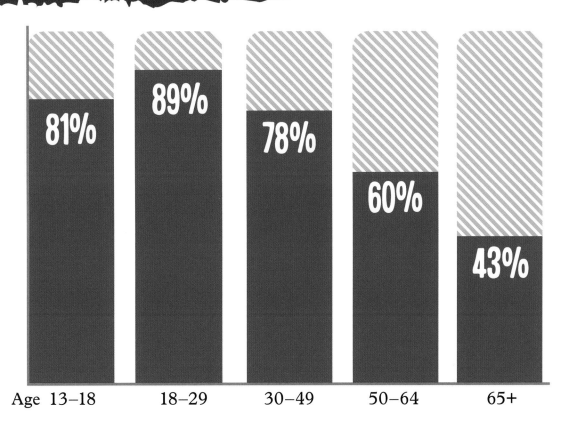

81%	89%	78%	60%	43%
Age 13–18	18–29	30–49	50–64	65+

How much time are kids your
age spending on social media
or watching videos on sites
such as YouTube?

**Ages 8 to 12 average
6 hours per day.**

**Ages 13 to 18 average
9 hours per day.**

KIDS AND MOBILE DEVICES

Households with kids tend to go mobile. Check out the statistics comparing households with kids to households without them.

88% of households with kids have smartphones.

68% of households without kids have smartphones.

45% of households without kids have tablets.

70% of households with kids have tablets.

Do you remember your first time online? You may not. Today babies are even going online! According to a 2015 survey of American parents regarding children **under age 1:**

52% have watched TV.

36% have touched or scrolled a screen.

24% have made a call from a cell phone.

15% have used an app.

12% have played a video game.

CHANGING TRENDS IN MOBILE DEVICES

Statistics show that kids in the United States are using mobile devices at younger ages than just a few years ago. They also have more privacy with their screens than ever before.

	2012	2016
Average age at which someone under 18 gets first cell phone	**12** years old	**10.3** years old
Percent of people under 18 who have access to the Internet with their own device	**42%**	**64%**
Percent of people under 18 who use Internet from room shared by their family (living room, office, den)	**85%**	**76%**
Percent of people under 18 who use Internet from their own rooms	**15%**	**24%**
Percent of people under 18 who prefer to use a tablet during car rides	**26%**	**55%**
Percent of people under 18 who prefer to use smartphone during car rides	**36%**	**45%**

TEENS AND MOBILE DEVICES

You know better than anyone that kids your age are on the go!
It's probably no surprise that 91% of American teens ages 13-17
use mobile devices to go online.

What percentage
of teens have
access to:

 = smartphone

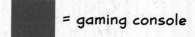 = computer

= tablet

= gaming console

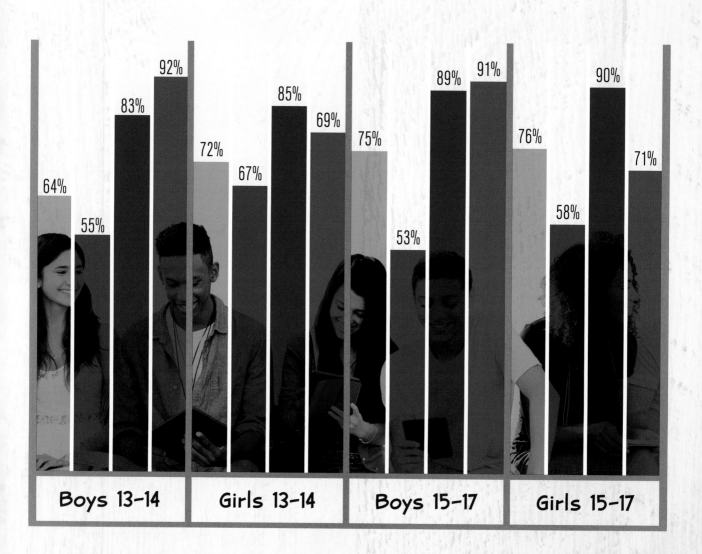

Boys 13-14: 64% · 55% · 83% · 92%

Girls 13-14: 72% · 67% · 85% · 69%

Boys 15-17: 75% · 53% · 89% · 91%

Girls 15-17: 76% · 58% · 90% · 71%

TEENS AND PHONE OWNERSHIP

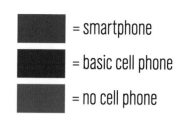

= smartphone
= basic cell phone
= no cell phone

By Age

	smartphone	basic cell phone	no cell phone
All Teens	73%	15%	12%
Ages 13 to 14	68%	14%	18%
Ages 15 to 17	76%	16%	8%

By Ethnicity

	smartphone	basic cell phone	no cell phone
White	71%	17%	12%
Black	85%	7%	8%
Hispanic	71%	15%	14%

By Location

	smartphone	basic cell phone	no cell phone
Urban	73%	16%	11%
Suburban	74%	14%	12%
Rural	68%	16%	15%

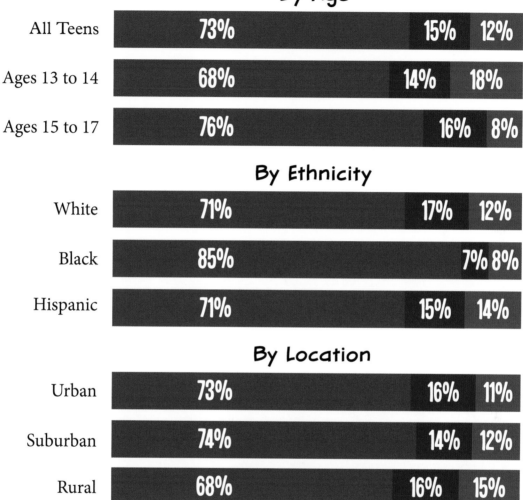

How does your phone use compare to other people your age? According to Pew Research in 2015, of Americans between the ages of **13 and 17**:

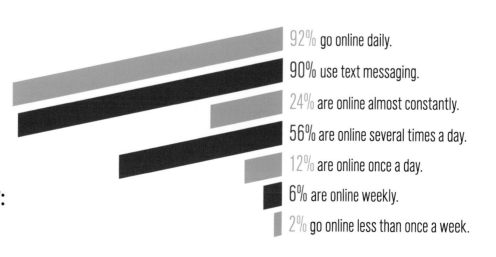

92% go online daily.

90% use text messaging.

24% are online almost constantly.

56% are online several times a day.

12% are online once a day.

6% are online weekly.

2% go online less than once a week.

TEXTING IS TOPS

Texting, whether it's through social media or directly from phone to phone, is overwhelmingly preferred by teens as a means of communication. In 2015 the New York Times found that teens send, on average, 60 texts per day. Girls send closer to 100 texts, and boys send around 50. How do your texting habits compare?

AGES

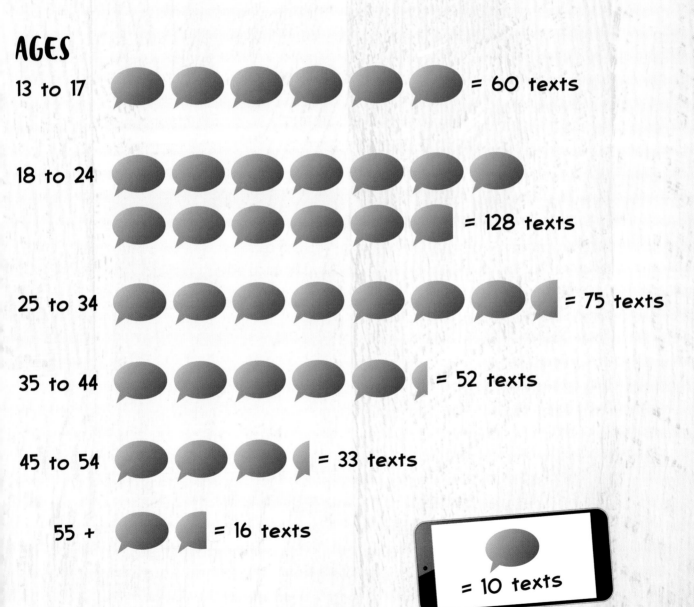

13 to 17 = 60 texts

18 to 24 = 128 texts

25 to 34 = 75 texts

35 to 44 = 52 texts

45 to 54 = 33 texts

55 + = 16 texts

= 10 texts

Texting is great! It's quicker than calling someone, and you can message multiple people at the same time. But you knew that. You might not know these fun factoids.

90 seconds: the average response time for a text.

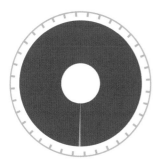

99% of texts are read.

95% of texts are read within 3 minutes of being sent.

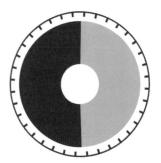

51% of teens would rather communicate digitally than in person.

TEXTING VERSUS PHONE CALLS

So with all this texting, is anyone actually talking to each other on their phones?

 Yes, but it's getting less and less.

26 minutes: the amount of time an average American spends a day texting

6 minutes: the amount of time the average American spends talking on the phone

88 the number of text messages Americans ages 18-29 send per day

17 the number of phone calls Americans ages 18-29 make per day

Chapter 2

SOCIAL MEDIA PLATFORMS

Social media platforms have come a long way in the last 20 years. The first one was created in 1997. It was called Six Degrees. Today there are countless social media sites, but a few are the most popular with teens. Instagram and Snapchat are at the top of the heap.

WHAT SOCIAL MEDIA PLATFORMS DO TEENS USE?

* Data is based on teens aged 13 to 17.

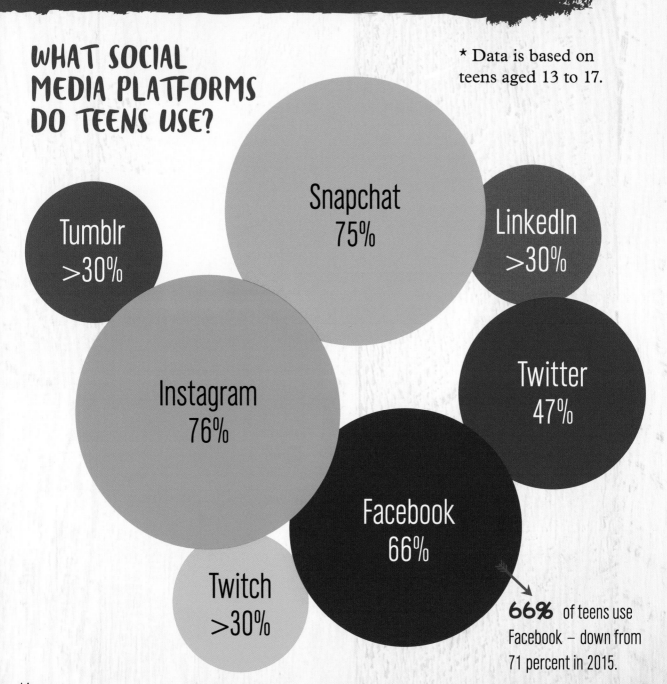

Tumblr >30%

Snapchat 75%

LinkedIn >30%

Instagram 76%

Twitter 47%

Facebook 66%

Twitch >30%

66% of teens use Facebook – down from 71 percent in 2015.

WHAT ARE THE RESTRICTIONS?

Social media sites have minimum age standards.
Do you know what they are?

Twitter Reddit Facebook Snapchat Instagram Steam Pinterest Twitch Google+ Path	YouTube WeChat Foursquare Flickr Kik	LinkedIn	WhatsApp
age: **13**	**13** (w/parents' permission)	**14**	**16**

A 2016 survey by the British news program Newsround reported that 75% of British kids between ages 10 and 12 have social media accounts. This is below the required age limits.

MOST POPULAR SOCIAL MEDIA PLATFORMS FOR TEENS BY GENDER

67.9% 66.7% 47.7% 34.9% 40.3%

Teen Girls

Instagram ▪

Snapchat ▪

Facebook ▪

Twitter ▪

Google+ ▪

51.9% 46.6% 57.6% 35.9% 44%

Teen Boys

MILLIONS AND BILLIONS

Social media users flood cyberspace with text messages, videos, and posts. The numbers surrounding various media platforms may astound you. They reach into the millions and even billions!

Instagram

300 million
selfies posted

500 million
active monthly users

$1.53 billion
made from advertisers every year

4.2 billion
posts liked every day

40 billion
photographs uploaded since 2010

95 million
photos and videos shared every day

YouTube

3.25 billion
hours of video watched each month

1 billion
mobile video views per day

Snapchat

1 million snaps
created every day

100 million
daily users

300+ million
active monthly users

400+ million
Snapchat stories
created every day

10+ billion
Snapchat video views daily

Twitter

- **23 million** fake accounts
- **310 million** monthly users
- **500 million** tweets sent each day
- **500 million** monthly visits
  without logging in
- **1.3 billion accounts**
  created since 2006

Facebook

16 million small businesses with Facebook pages

83 million fake profiles

300 million photos uploaded every day

1.15 billion mobile daily active users

1.32 billion users log on daily

2.01 billion active users worldwide

Chapter 3
SOCIAL MEDIA SAVVY

Test your social media IQ with these fast facts. Did you know that two of the three top visited websites are social media sites? They are Google, Facebook, and YouTube. See if any of these other facts surprise you.

You can navigate YouTube in 76 different languages.

Every minute, 510,000 comments are posted on Facebook.

More than 20,000 photos are shared on Snapchat every second.

There are 300 hours of video uploaded to YouTube every minute.

Five new Facebook profiles are created every second.

Instagram users from Makati City and Pasig, Philippines, take the most "selfies" — 258 per 100,000 people.

"Charlie bit my finger" is the user-submitted YouTube video with the most views.

Every minute, 136,000 photos are uploaded to Facebook.

It would take 10 years to view all the photos put on Snapchat in 1 hour.

Every minute, 293,000 statuses are updated on Facebook.

In Nice, France, there are 30 selfie-takers per 100,000 people. The city is 100th on the list of cities with the most selfie-takers.

PINBOARDS, DISCUSSION BOARDS, AND BLOGS

Pinboards are online sites such as Pinterest and Polyvore. Users "pin" visual content to create displays. Discussion boards such as Reddit or Digg provide a place for users to exchange opinions or mini-blogs.

FUN PINTEREST FACTS

175 million active monthly users

The average pin is repinned **11 times**.

There are more than **75 billion** pins on **1.5 billion boards.**

85% of users are female.

12% of Pinterest searches contain a spelling error.

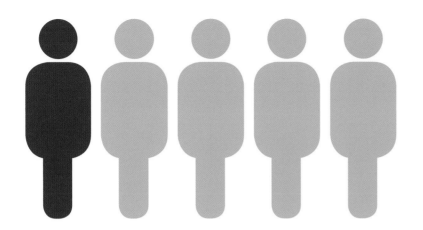

One in five teens uses pinboards.

17% »»>

of teens read
or comment on
discussion boards
such as Reddit or Digg.

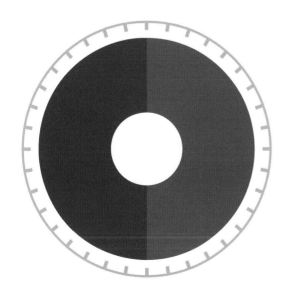

An equal number of
boys and girls visit
discussion boards.

SOCIAL MEDIA STARS

Teens who have huge followings on social media are called digital influencers. Will you be the next big star?

TEEN SOCIAL MEDIA STARS OF 2017

Name	Famous for	Age	Platforms	Followers
Emily Bear	musician and composer	15	Twitter	18,200
Hanna Alper	blogger	14	Twitter	40,000
Jazz Jennings	transgender role model	16	YouTube	357,000
Jake Mitchell	vlogger	17	YouTube	1.7 million
Amanda Steele	fashion and beauty	18	YouTube Twitter	2.8 million 1.06 million
Jacob Sartorius	singer	14	Instagram YouTube	8.4 million 2.6 million
"Matty B" (Matthew Morris)	remixing videos	14	Facebook YouTube	8.5 million 9.1 million

*Numbers current as of October 2017.

Jacob Sartorius

Amanda Steele

Jazz Jennings

Emily Bear

Jake Mitchell

"Matty B"

Hanna Alper

MOST TWITTER FOLLOWERS OF 2017

 = 1 million followers

Katy Perry
105 million
followers

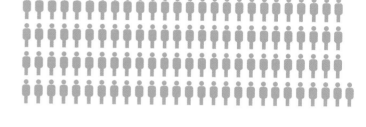

Justin Bieber
103 million
followers

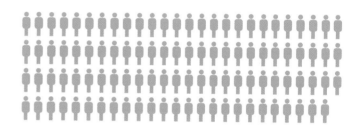

Barack Obama
96.3 million
followers

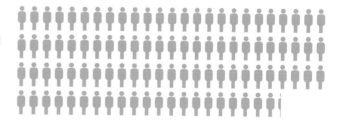

Taylor Swift
85.6 million
followers

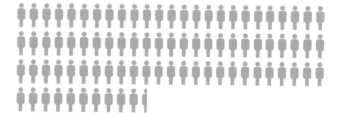

Rihanna
80.9 million
followers

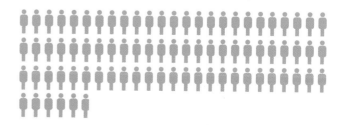

MEMES

Have you heard the saying, "A picture is worth a thousand words?" Memes take that idea to the next level. These photos or videos are paired with text that can be funny, political, or informational. You've probably seen tons of them. Anyone can make a meme, and they are passed from person to person. The best of the best go viral.

BEHIND THE MEMES

Memes are a hoot! But have you ever wondered about the people or animals in them? They're more than just an image. So who are they?

Grumpy Cat
Real Name: Tardar Sauce
Birthdate: April 4, 2012
Tardar Sauce took the internet by storm in 2012. Her grumpy expression paired with text such as, "I had fun once … It was awful," inspired many more feline lovers to create funny memes of their cranky kitties.

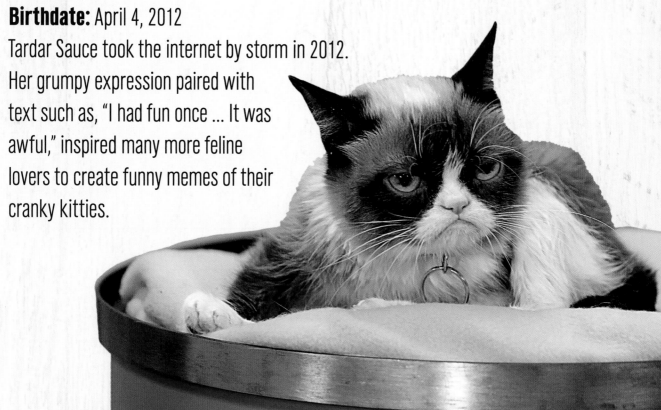

Bad Luck Brian

Real Name: Kyle Craven

Birthdate: August 10, 1989

Kyle Craven's friends got hold of one of his high school photos, and it set the internet on fire! Photo captions with "Bad Luck Brian" often muse about awful luck. For example, "Goes surfing for the first time … hurricane." The Bad Luck Brian meme became so popular that Kyle created a Bad Luck Brian Youtube channel. As of October 2017, it had more than 56,500 subscribers.

Success Kid

Real Name: Sammy Griner

Birthdate: September 23, 2006

Surely you've seen the cute toddler in the white and green t-shirt pumping his fist. His face often accompanies words of unlikely accomplishments. One example is "See a nickel on the ground … actually a silver dollar." Sammy's family used the popularity of the meme to fundraise $100,000 to pay for his father's kidney transplant surgery in 2015.

ATTENTION GAMERS

Video games have been around for decades, but interactive online gaming lets gamers interact with each other all over the world.

59% of all teen girls play video games online or on their phones.

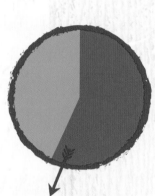

57% of all teen boys have made friends online while playing games.

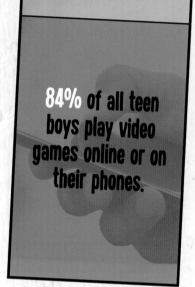

84% of all teen boys play video games online or on their phones.

13% of all teen girls have made friends online while playing games.

Gaming is big business, and it's projected to grow in the future. According to a worldwide study done by newzoo.com, the gaming market will grow more than $25 BILLION between 2016 and 2020. Most of this increase is due to increased use of smartphones for gaming.

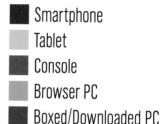

- ■ Smartphone
- □ Tablet
- ■ Console
- ■ Browser PC
- ■ Boxed/Downloaded PC

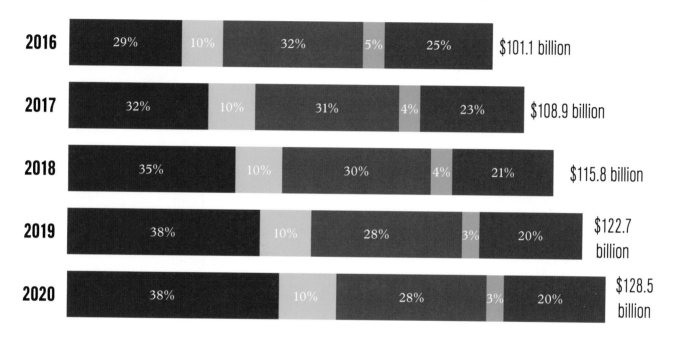

Year	Smartphone	Tablet	Console	Browser PC	Boxed/Downloaded PC	Total
2016	29%	10%	32%	5%	25%	$101.1 billion
2017	32%	10%	31%	4%	23%	$108.9 billion
2018	35%	10%	30%	4%	21%	$115.8 billion
2019	38%	10%	28%	3%	20%	$122.7 billion
2020	38%	10%	28%	3%	20%	$128.5 billion

POKEMON IN FIGURES

Pokemon Go took the world by storm when it came out in 2016.

290 million: total sales through March 2017 in units worldwide

11: number of languages the trading card game is printed in

74: number of countries and regions the trading card game is sold in

98: countries and regions where the animated TV show airs

VIDEOS ON SOCIAL MEDIA

Videos are a growing part of social media. Sites such as YouTube were made purely for the purposes of sharing videos, but video sharing is now an option on virtually every social media platform.

By 2019:
80% of Internet traffic around the world will involve videos.

1 million minutes

of videos are shared online every **second.**
That's **3.6 billion videos** per hour.

It would take
5 million years

to watch all the videos shared online in a month. To put that into perspective, that would be
50,000 centuries!

YOUTUBE BASICS

Founded in 2004

Users watch 3.2 billion hours of YouTube videos each month.

1.5 billion logged-in monthly users

180.1 million people in the U.S. use YouTube.

U.S. TEENS ON YOUTUBE

91%
91% of U.S. internet users ages 13-17 use YouTube.

77%
77% of teens subscribe to a YouTube channel.

64%
64% of teens share YouTube videos on Facebook.

50%
50% of teens look for YouTube videos that are funny.

49%
49% of teens have uploaded a YouTube video.

31

SHARING MUSIC ON SOCIAL MEDIA

Social music sites bring you your favorite music and let you share it with your friends. Pandora and YouTube are two of the most popular sites for sharing music.

PANDORA STATS

P = 1 million people

PPPPPPPPPPPPPPPPPPPPPPP
PPPPPPPPPPPPPPPPPPPPPPP
PPPPPPPPPPPPPPPPPPPPPPP
PPPPPP

Pandora has **81 million** monthly active listeners. Of those, **4.4 million** are subscribers.

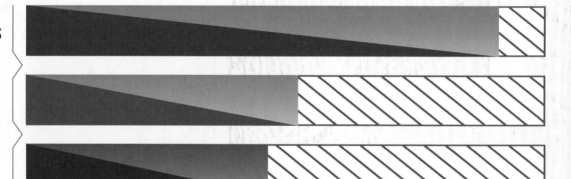

91%
of Pandora listeners use mobile devices.

52%
Female Listeners

48%
Male Listeners

In 2016 Pandora listeners played nearly **22 billion** hours worth of music.

GETTING MUSICAL

Musical.ly is especially popular with teens. This site lets you create your own music videos to your favorite tunes.

MUSICAL.LY STATS

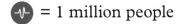 = 1 million people

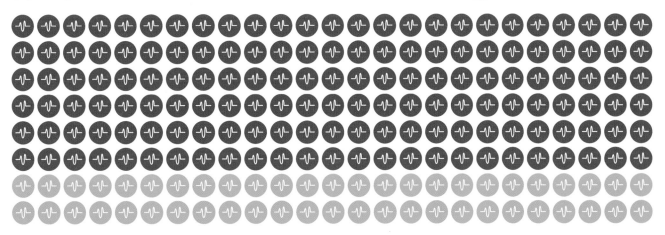

As of 2017, Musical.ly had **200 million** users.
Of those users, 50 million were under the age of 21.

49%
of Musical.ly users are in the U.S.

70%
Female Listeners

30%
Male Listeners

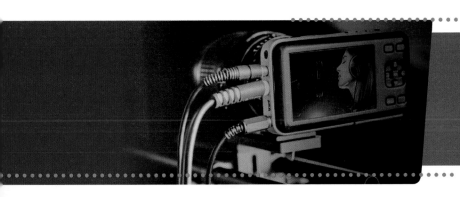

About **13 million** videos are uploaded to Musical.ly each day.

THE ECONOMICS OF SOCIAL MEDIA

Social media is big business for advertisers. More and more advertising dollars are being spent on social media every year.

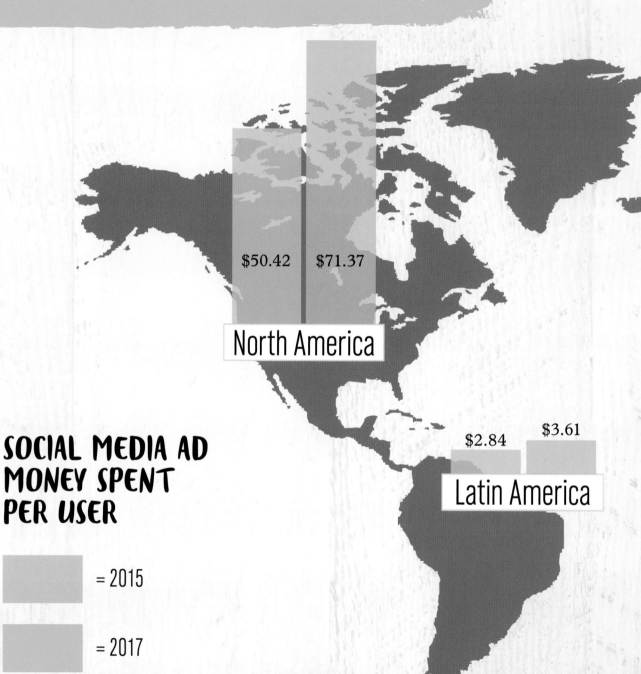

$50.42 $71.37

North America

SOCIAL MEDIA AD
MONEY SPENT
PER USER

$2.84 $3.61

Latin America

= 2015

= 2017

The advertising money spent on social media has
made these businesses **BILLIONS** of dollars!

Social Media Site	Year Founded	Estimated Worth
Snapchat	2011	$15.25 billion
Twitter	2006	$11.82 billion
Facebook and Instagram (jointly owned)	2004	$489.62 billion

*numbers current as of August 3, 2017

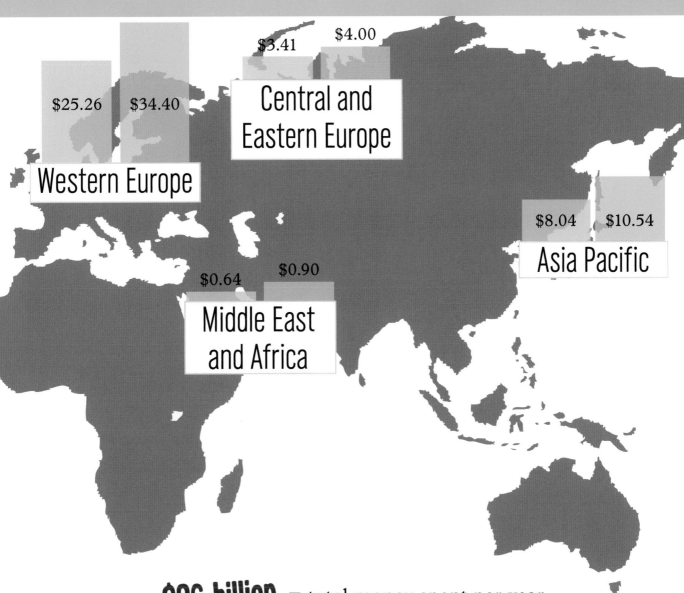

$3.41 $4.00

$25.26 $34.40

Central and
Eastern Europe

Western Europe

$8.04 $10.54

Asia Pacific

$0.64 $0.90

Middle East
and Africa

$36 billion = total money spent per year
by advertisers on social media

Chapter 4

PROTECT YOUR ONLINE PRIVACY

Only **9%** of teens claim to be worried about privacy on social media.

However, **60%** keep their Facebook setting private.

SIX WAYS TO PROTECT YOUR PRIVACY ONLINE:

1. Use social media privacy settings.
2. Only communicate with people on social media who you know in real life.
3. Don't log in to other websites using your social media log-ins. Once you do, those websites can access your information.
4. Don't reveal personal information, such as your last name, phone number, or home address.
5. Log out when you leave a social media website.
6. Remember that whatever you post online may be seen by strangers as well as people you know.

WHAT ARE YOU SHARING?

Everything you share online tells people something about yourself. See how your posts compare to those of other teens.

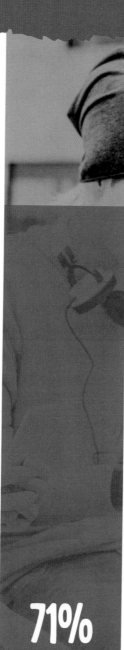

91% pics of themselves

71% their school's name

71% the city or town where they live

53% email address

20% cell phone number

WATCH OUT FOR SCAMMERS AND HACKERS!

By now you probably know that there are dishonest people out there who try to steal or cheat people out of money or information. Hackers are people who use computers to obtain a person's or company's information and data. Scammers use dishonest tricks to steal money.

In 2016 hackers used social media to steal or cheat people out of $2.5 billion! Here's the breakdown:

$60 million
DropBox

$117 million
From LinkedIn

$350 million
MySpace

$65 million
Tumblr

$412 million
FriendFinder Network

$1.5 billion
Yahoo email

ALERT:

If you receive a "friend request" on social media from someone who is already a friend, it may be a scammer. Scammers recreate your friend's profile, photos, and "About" information. Do not accept the request without double checking with your friend — preferably in the real world.

A 2016 University of Phoenix study found that 2/3 of adults said their social media accounts have been hacked. What have they done to protect themselves?

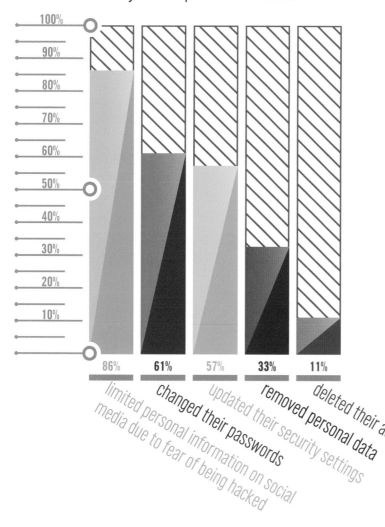

Percentage	Action
86%	limited personal information on social media due to fear of being hacked
61%	changed their passwords
57%	updated their security settings
33%	removed personal data
11%	deleted their account completely

TIPS FOR TEENS

It's important to avoid scams and hackers. Here are some tips:

1. Avoid using public WiFi spots. It's easy for hackers to access your data.
2. Don't share passwords. Choose passwords that are hard to guess. Change them often.
3. Don't respond to pop-up ads or unknown emails. Never click on links attached to an email if you do not know the sender.
4. Don't click on links. It's safer to type the website address into your browser.
5. Be sure your computer or smartphone has anti-virus software.

CYBERBULLYING

Cyberbullying is a real problem with teens. In a 2016 survey of 5,707 U.S. students ages 12 to 17, students reported that:

33.8%	had been a victim of cyberbullying at some time in their lives
22.5%	had seen mean or hurtful comments online
20.1%	had read rumors online
12.7%	had seen posts about themselves containing mean names or sexually explicit content
12.2%	had been threatened online
10.3%	had their identity used online by others without their consent
10.1%	had seen mean comments online about their race or ethnicity
7.4%	had a mean or hurtful video about them posted online
7.1%	had seen a mean or hurtful web page made about them
10.3%	had skipped school because of online bullying

60% of students felt that online bullying affected their ability to learn and feel safe!

COMBAT CYBERBULLIES!

If you or a friend are ever the target of a cyberbully, **ConnectSafely.org** offers some tips to help.

1. Don't respond. Sometimes the best thing to do is ignore the bully.

2. Don't retaliate. That just keeps the cycle of bullying going.

3. Save the evidence. Proof is power, especially if the bullying gets serious enough that you need to go to the authorities.

4. Talk to a trusted adult. They can be there to back you up and help you decide how to handle the situation.

5. Block the bully. If you can change your privacy settings to get a bully out of your life, do it!

6. Be civil. Even if you don't like someone, it's always best to be the bigger person. Don't sink to the level of a bully.

7. Don't BE the bully. Think before you post something on social media or text message someone. Would you be hurt if someone said the same thing about or to you?

8. Be a friend, not a bystander. Stand up to bullies! Don't forward on their messages or share cruel posts.

Chapter 5

DIGITAL DANGERS AND DISTRACTIONS

Could you be addicted to social media? Do you feel like you can't put your phone down? You're not alone!

72%

teens who feel the need to respond immediately to texts or other messages

78%

teens who check their devices hourly

50%

teens who feel they are addicted to their mobile devices

66%

parents who feel their teens spend too much time on their devices

69%

parents who check their devices hourly

22%

teens who feel their parents are addicted to their devices

SLEEP DEPRIVATION

A 2016 British study of students ages 12 to 15 showed that 1 in 5 got up during the night to check their mobile devices. That same year, a group of British university researchers found that using smartphones or tablets before bedtime doubles the risk of a poor night's sleep.

THE DANGERS OF DISTRACTION

330,000:
the number of car accidents caused by texting each year

11,100 :
the number of injuries caused by distracted walking while using cell phones from 2000 to 2011

Every time you text behind the wheel, you're
23 times
more likely to cause an accident than if you keep the phone turned off.

21% of teens killed in car accidents were using a cell phone at the time.

52% of teens talk on the phone while driving.

94% of teens say they know it's a bad idea to text and drive.

But **35%** of them do it anyway.

11 teens die every day in texting-and-driving accidents.

YUCK! THAT'S GROSS!

Social media communities provide hours of fun. But did you know thriving communities of germs live on your smartphone? Check out these dirty facts.

Newsflash: Your cell phone is 10 times more germ-ridden than most toilet seats.

BAD BATHROOM HABITS

You wouldn't believe what some people admit to doing with their phones in the bathroom.

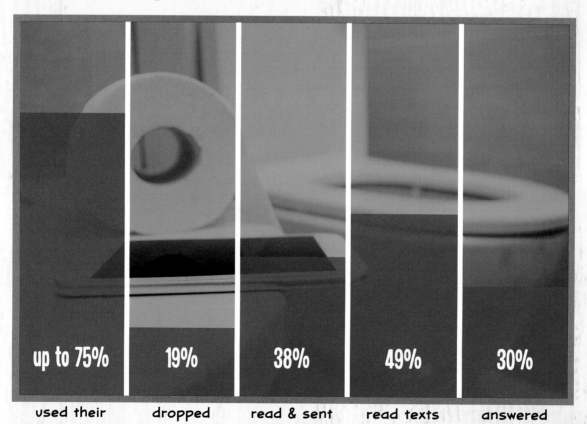

up to 75%	19%	38%	49%	30%
used their phone in the bathroom	dropped phone in the toilet	read & sent emails while on the toilet	read texts while on the toilet	answered phone while on the toilet

GERMS PER SQUARE INCH

You might be surprised to find out what the germiest places and items in your home are. Then again you may not be. Where did you expect your cell phone to show up in the order?

Common Household Items	Germs Per Square Inch
computer mouse	50
computer keyboard	64
TV remote	70
toilet flush handle	83
toilet seat	295
kitchen counter	488
bathroom floor in front of toilet	764
kitchen floor in front of sink	830
kitchen faucet handle	13,227
cell phone	**25,000**
kitchen sponge	134,630

RECIPE FOR A CLEAN PHONE

You will need:
8 ounces of 70% rubbing alcohol OR 8 ounces of white vinegar
8 ounces of distilled water*

1. Mix the liquids in a small spray bottle.
2. Spray a soft cloth and wipe down the phone.
3. Use a cotton swab or a toothpick to clean the gunk out of the cracks between the glass cover and the phone's case.

Do this often. Your phone will be much safer!

* You must use distilled water. Tap water can leave a residue on the phone.

USING SOCIAL MEDIA FOR GOOD

It's true that social media can be hurtful, harmful, or downright dangerous when used at the wrong time or in the wrong way. But does that mean it's necessarily a bad thing? No way! Aside from being a fun way to stay connected, a lot of good has been done through social media. It has been used widely to raise money for good causes. This recent phenomenon is called crowdfunding.

POPULAR CROWDFUNDING SITES

DonorsChoose raises funds for underfunded public schools.

GoFundMe raises funds for personal or charitable projects.

KickStarter raises funds for creative projects.

Indiegogo raises funds for artists, musicians, and others to complete projects.

Fundable raises funds to start new businesses.

GOFUNDME SUCCESS STORIES: HELPING OTHERS

The parents of four-year-old Eliza O'Neill, who was diagnosed with a genetic disease, raise nearly $1 million. They use the money to fund a clinical drug trial that could save their daughter's life. To date, they have raised more than $2 million.

Las Vegas Sheriff Joe Lombardo raised $8.7 million in just two days to help the victims of the October 2017 shooting in Las Vegas.

GoFundMe is founded.

2010

2013

2017

2013

Friends of Boston Marathon bombing victim John Bauman launch a campaign in his honor. They raise more than $800,000 to help with medical expenses.

2016

Equality Florida launches a GoFundMe campaign that raises nearly $8 million for the victims of the Pulse shooting in Orlando, Florida.

Author Bio

   Elizabeth Raum is a full-time writer who has lived in 12 different cities and towns in 7 different states. She currently lives in Fargo, North Dakota (population 120,762, which is 15% of the state's total population). Her favorite ways to stay in touch with friends and family are face-to-face visits, email, talking on the phone, texting, and social media. She is fascinated by statistics and hopes you are too. To learn more, visit her website at www.elizabethraum.net.

Books in This Set

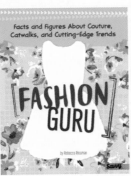

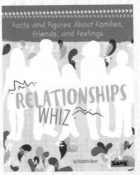